Shattered not Broken

Like the Phoenix, I Rise

BY CLARICE JENKINS

Shattered not Broken

Like the Phoenix, I Rise

CLARICE JENKINS

StoryTerrace

Design Mitar Stjepcevic, on behalf of StoryTerrace

Copyright © Clarice Jenkins and StoryTerrace

Text is private and confidential

First print July 2022

StoryTerrace

www.StoryTerrace.com

CONTENTS

1. CEREMONY IN BLUE (MAY 3RD, 2022) — 7
2. HAMPTONVILLE (1977-1989) — 13
3. LIFE AFTER GRANDDADDY (1989-1995) — 21
4. FINDING MY WAY (1995-2003) — 29
5. A MAN NAMED JEWEL (1955-2003) — 39
6. HAPPY TOGETHER (2003-2011) — 51
7. JACE (2011-2017) — 63
8. BATTLING CANCER (2017-2020) — 75
9. SAYING GOODBYE (2020) — 85
10. RISING FROM THE ASHES (2020-PRESENT) — 93

Empire State Building Lights for Police Memorial Day 2022

1

CEREMONY IN BLUE
(MAY 3RD, 2022)

On May 3rd, 2022, I woke up a few blocks away from New York City's World Trade Center in the Marriott Residence Inn. My 10-year-old son, Jace, and I were dressed in shades of blue—he in a navy blue and gray shirt, and I in a royal blue dress. We stepped out of our hotel into the cool morning and met my two stepsons, Jewel Bobby and Christopher (who I call my "bonus sons"), as well as Jewel Bobby's two sons. Together, we went to New York City's Police Headquarters.

Although Jace and I had spent the past two days doing all the typical things that people do when they visit New York City, we had not traveled all the way from our home in South Carolina just to be tourists. The purpose of our trip was to attend a ceremony honoring 35 fallen NYPD officers whose names were being added to the "Hall of Heroes," a memorial wall in the lobby of Police Headquarters. One of them was Jewel Jenkins—my late husband and Jace's father, who'd died on May 24th, 2020. The date of the ceremony would have been his 67th birthday.

Convincing me to come had been an effort for my stepsons. Two years earlier, when Jewel had passed, I had sworn off New York City. As a first responder after the 9/11 attacks in 2001, Jewel had been exposed to dangerous toxins and suffered severe mental anguish. I couldn't help holding a vendetta against the city that felt like the reason he was gone. But once the ceremony commenced, I realized how grateful I was that we were there. The proceedings were brief but heavy with significance, with a quiet, somber atmosphere. Some of the attendees wept silently as the officers' names were called and their families were honored. Each member of our family wore blue, because blue was Jewel's favorite color.

After the ceremony, we and the other families boarded Mercedes Sprinter vans that drove us to the Empire State Building. With one police escort in front of our van and another behind us, we made quite the entrance. We were taken to the top, where the CEO of the Empire State Building presented Jace and Jewel Bobby's sons with teddy bears. Jace was given the privilege of turning on the landmark's famous lights alongside NYPD Commissioner Keechantt Sewell. That night, in memory of the fallen officers, the lights shone blue and purple.

Our final stop was One World Trade Center, for dinner at the top of America's tallest building. We were so high up that I had the sense we were dining in the sky. It was an unforgettable meal, but for me, it was also bittersweet. It seemed strange to celebrate Jewel's life in the location of the attack that eventually led to his death.

Of course, I appreciated the way Jewel's NYPD family honored him. Since Jewel's death, Jace and I have received a huge amount of support from his family in blue. Still, that bittersweet feeling followed me the whole day. We were being treated like royalty, whereas I'm used to blending into the background. From the news crews covering the ceremony to the police escorts leading and flanking our van, attention was lavished on us. And yet, what I wanted more than anything was for Jewel to be there with us. When the police commissioner called his name in the roll call during the ceremony, it struck me that his name would never again be called as a police officer in New York City.

At one point in the day, I got into a conversation with a woman whose husband had died within four days of mine. Like Jewel's, her husband's death was related to the 9/11 attacks on the World Trade Center. Like many others in the room, we'd found ourselves in the same strange club—widows or widowers of fallen heroes. Our significant others had paid the ultimate sacrifice, and that terrible moment in history had brought us all together.

The woman told me that she admired me because I was able to speak about Jewel without breaking down. I told her that I do cry for him, because I miss him. But I also know that I did absolutely everything in my power to keep him here on earth. If there were anything more I could have done, I would have done it.

Jace had the time of his life on that trip. It was his first time seeing the city where his father grew up and built his career. He got to spend time with his adoring half-brothers and Jewel Bobby's kids, who he's very close with. We went shopping, took the subway to Times Square, visited the Statue of Liberty, and rode the Staten Island Ferry. He got to sit in the copilot seat of the plane on our trip there, and he was given a second set of wings by the pilot on the way back. Still, none of that compared to witnessing the ceremony where his father was honored for his sacrifices.

Jewel retired when Jace was born, so Jace only knew him as a world-class stay-at-home dad. But in New York, he got to see that his father was also a hero without a cape.

Over the course of his career in law enforcement, Jewel received a number of plaques and certificates broadcasting his accomplishments, but he kept them hidden in a box in the basement. He never wanted accolades or recognition; for him, performing his duties with excellence was simply doing his job. These past two years, I have started hanging those awards on the walls of my house. I always bragged about Jewel, because he would never do it for himself. I guess I'm still doing that now.

In addition to the Hall of Heroes, Jewel's name was added to a memorial wall in Albany on May 10th, and his name appears on memorial walls at the World Trade Center, the Battery, Long Island, and Washington, D.C. I'm thankful for these honors, because they help show the world what a special and important individual he was. It is my hope and my mission that Jewel Jenkins' name will never be forgotten.

All roads led to Hamptonville

2

HAMPTONVILLE (1977–1989)

My story began a long way from the bright lights of New York City. I grew up in Pinewood, South Carolina, on 28 acres of land purchased in 1970 by my paternal grandparents, Powell Hampton Senior and Rosa Odell (called Dell by everyone who knew her). My grandparents raised 11 children on that land, and seven of them ended up raising their families there as well. My grandparents christened it "the homestead," but the rest of our town called it "Hamptonville."

My grandparents came from humble beginnings. My grandfather served in the military, then became a pastor. According to my grandmother, he seemed like a highly unlikely candidate to lead a congregation when he was younger. As she put it, he was a little rough around the collar. But he made a decision to change and live differently. Following the lead of his parents, he became more involved in church and eventually went into the ministry.

I was born to Charlie and Katherine Hampton on January 18th, 1977. My younger sister, Kayla, was born on September 18th, 1981. According to my parents, I was not happy when they brought her home from the hospital. As the story goes, I thought she was coming to replace me, so I tormented her as a baby. But before long, Kayla became my best friend. To this day, she and I are extremely close. She's my sounding board, and I'm hers.

My parents made sure Kayla and I were well fed and well educated, but they never spoiled us. Instead, they instilled a sense of responsibility in us by establishing an expectation of reciprocity. Rather than simply giving us things, they showed us how to earn them. They let us know that we would be rewarded only if we followed their rules and met certain standards, and they taught us not to be materialistic and to appreciate what we had.

Both my dad and my mom looked up to my father's parents. My mother has always been grateful to them and seen them in a parental role, because her own parents were largely absent in her life. Although they were married when she was born, they divorced and moved away when she was a young child, leaving her maternal grandparents to raise her and her five younger siblings. In many ways, my mother regards her grandparents as her real parents. When they passed, she paid for their tombstones, and she still goes to the cemetery to visit them. Even though being abandoned by her parents scarred her significantly, she's grateful for the upbringing her grandparents gave her.

Like my dad, my mother grew up in Sumter County in South Carolina, but on the opposite side of the county. They met as young teenagers and became high school sweethearts. My dad finished high school, but my mom had to drop out before graduation and work to support herself and her siblings. As a young person, she thought she would lose my dad as a result of that sacrifice, but to her surprise, he stayed by her side and taught her what she had missed in the classes she didn't get to take. They got married in 1974.

When Kayla and I were young children, my mom worked at a local sewing factory, but her allergies and sinuses caused a lot of problems during her employment there, and eventually, she had to quit. She started substituting at the local school district, then took a job as a cafeteria worker. Later, she worked for the school system in other roles, on the custodial team and as a bus aide helping disabled children board and disembark the bus.

My dad worked as a supervisor at a local battery plant when I was young, but he always felt a sense of expectation that he would follow in his father's footsteps and become a pastor. When he was a child, several congregants in his church had predicted that he would go into the ministry one day, and deep down, he knew it was true. Still, before he pursued it, he wanted to receive divine confirmation. Eventually, he did.

In 2003, Dad was diagnosed with colon cancer. He prayed and asked God to heal him, promising that if God cured him, he would commit the rest of his life to the ministry. He underwent surgery, and since then, he has never needed chemo or other any other subsequent treatment. God cured him, so he fulfilled his end of the bargain. He's been cancer-free and preaching ever since. For the past six years, he has been working at a church in Charleston.

***

My house and the homes of the other six siblings who stayed on the homestead all started as mobile homes, then were eventually transformed into permanent homes. Each family's lot was approximately an acre, so we each had some of our own space, but still, I grew up surrounded by Hamptons.

I've always been close with my aunts and uncles who lived on the homestead. Growing up, I saw them day in, day out and obeyed them like I obeyed my parents. But the best part of growing up there was having my cousins all nearby. There are 29 cousins in my generation, and we have always had a special connection. With the exception of the children of my dad's oldest brother, who moved to New Jersey, the rest of us were raised either at the homestead or in the local area. Our elementary school had kindergarten through eighth grade, so we all rode the bus there together, and we filled up half of it. We knew everyone in our community, and everyone knew us.

To this day, my cousins and I are uniquely intertwined. Many of our birthdays fall in January and September, so we consider those the birthday months. During those months, there are birthdays just about every day. There have never been exclusive groups among us. We're all fiercely protective of one another, and although we might criticize each other at times, no one outside of our family is allowed to do that. Currently, the eldest cousin is 56, and the youngest is 21. I am somewhere in the middle, with some of the crew ahead of me and the majority behind me. Together, we had a wonderful childhood.

Ironically, my cousins and I always dreamed about escaping the country. The TV shows we watched made cities and the suburbs look so much more exciting than the rural life we knew. But now when we look back, we're grateful. We made so many special memories. In the summer we would hold fireworks competitions, splitting into two groups and going to opposite sides of the property to shoot bottle rockets and see if they'd meet in the sky. We loved playing basketball on the court we had on the property, and sometimes we'd have championships against other local families. We would play all day, drinking water straight from the hose when we got thirsty in the hot sun. My grandmother would come out and bring out peanut butter and jelly sandwiches for everyone.

Grandma was the matriarch of our entire family. Even though Granddaddy was a cook during the years he served in the army, she always cooked at home. Most of the time, she didn't allow him in the kitchen because she said he made such a mess. She also didn't like his proclivity for wild, gamey meats, like rabbit.

My grandma's meals were unforgettable. She cooked fried chicken, collard greens, and perlo rice. She baked hot water cornbread, biscuits, apple cobbler, and an incredible pear cobbler that she made with the harvest from the pear trees on the property. She was also a Kool-Aid connoisseur, mixing flavor packets to create her own special combinations.

There were vegetable gardens on the homestead, and my family made them a source of fun competition. Even now, my dad and his brothers compete to see who can grow the largest watermelon, cantaloupe, collard greens, turnips, scallions, lima beans, and squash. The family eats what we want and need, and then the surplus is given to people in the community who need it.

We had animals, too. Granddaddy loved them, and he had a special gift for taking care of them. Although he was never trained as a veterinarian, he seemed to inherently know how to care for animals. When our neighbors' animals were sick, they would call him to come over and help them, because he always knew what to do. He raised cows and pigs for meat, and every Christmas, he would roast a pig on a spit for our Christmas dinner. He also raised chickens so we could use their eggs, as well as ducks, geese, guinea fowls, and peacocks. He had a horse, and there were always dogs, cats, and rabbits running around.

Because Granddaddy was a pastor, church was a major part of our lives. Every Sunday, the entire family went to church together, and afterward, we would go home, change out of our church clothes, and us kids would play until dark while my grandmother cooked a huge Sunday dinner. Our church, Antioch Reform Methodist Episcopal Church, was just five minutes down the road.

Members of Reformed Methodist Union Episcopal (RMUE) churches attend a local home church, but when someone accepts a calling to enter the ministry, they are assigned to a different church by the bishop. Because Granddaddy was a pastor, he was always assigned to work at a different church, so he spent Sunday mornings elsewhere, although he always found a way to spent Easter service at our home church. The furthest church he was assigned to was two hours away. He hated driving on the interstate, so he would drive the whole way on local roads.

I'm grateful that my faith was established when I was so young, because that faith has helped me and given me strength at points when life has tested me. Some of the things that have come my way would have made me crumple if it weren't for God.

Even though I had a firm foundation of faith as a child, it was tested when I was 12 years old. On Christmas Eve of 1989, my life changed forever.

3

LIFE AFTER GRANDDADDY (1989-1995)

My grandfather and I had an incredibly special bond. Part of the reason was that, until 1980, I was the only granddaughter in the family who lived in Hamptonville.

Granddaddy was born with only one kidney, and when he was 57, that kidney started to fail him. He had to start getting dialysis, which he did three times a week for almost my entire childhood.

On December 20th, 1989, my sister had a Christmas performance at school. The whole family attended to support her, but Granddaddy didn't go because he wasn't feeling well. When we got home, my grandmother asked my dad to take Grandaddy to the emergency room. My dad drove him there, and they kept him at the hospital. That wasn't particularly alarming, because, being on dialysis, Granddaddy often had to spend a few days at the hospital to build up his strength. When he came home, he always seemed perfectly fine. I assumed that this time would be like that, too.

Over the next few days, my dad's siblings kept coming to my house and having conversations too quiet for me to hear. I kept wondering what they were talking about. Then my mom told Kayla and me that we were going to stay with her mother for a few nights. I wanted to go to the hospital to see my grandpa, but they told me I was too young. The hospital required guests to be at least 12 years old, and I was 12, so I knew I would be allowed inside. However, my sister was too young, and because my parents always treated my sister and me the same way, they didn't let either of us go.

On Christmas Eve Day, there was a mandatory meeting at the hospital for my grandmother, my dad, and all of his siblings. Again, my parents dropped me and Kayla off at my maternal grandmother's house. While we were there, I noticed that my grandmother kept looking at me strangely, and I couldn't figure out why. Looking back as an adult, I realized that she must have known that things had gone downhill with my grandpa's health, but as a child, I didn't have an inkling.

Later, I learned that the meeting was held at the hospital because my grandfather was on life support. He had had a heart attack on the night of my sister's performance, and then while they were trying to treat him for the heart attack, he also suffered a stroke. He was placed on life support, and the doctors' tests showed no activity.

There was some disagreement among the siblings about whether to keep him on life support. Some of them claimed that they saw him moving, so they didn't want the life support to be taken off. Others said the only movement was a result of the machine. This caused a lot of tension between them. But eventually, Granddaddy was taken off life support and passed away on December 24th, 1989. He was only 67 years old.

***

The weeks and months following Granddaddy's death were extremely hard for my whole family. We were all devastated by the loss. Until then, we had never experienced that kind of collective loss, and it rocked us. We didn't know how to be in its wake. The day after he passed was Christmas Day, and all of his Christmas presents were under the tree. No one knew what to do with them. Some of my cousins decided to put their gifts in the casket with him.

My parents decided that my sister and I were too young to attend the funeral, so we stayed with my other grandmother. That still haunts me, because I wonder if I would have been able to process his death better if I had gone. Some of my older cousins went, and they didn't deal with it well, but there's no way to know how it would have affected me.

After that, I was angry. I was angry at my parents for shielding me from the truth about Grandaddy and not letting visit him at the hospital, but also at God Himself for letting this happen. Before that, my faith had been simple and childlike, but now, I was conflicted. I wondered if there was something I had done to deserve this, although I couldn't think what it might be. All of my family were good Christians. We went to church every Sunday, and I served as an usher and sang in the choir. The way I saw it, I was doing everything I was supposed to do. Why would God take my beloved grandfather, a pastor himself, on Christmas Eve of all days? To lose him was a debilitating blow, but to lose him on Christmas Eve, probably the most exciting night of the year for a child, was unimaginably painful.

I thank God for my grandmother, because my conversations with her helped me find a little more peace about his death. She told me that Granddaddy had been sick for a long time, and although he was never one to complain, he was very tired. She said that even though he was no longer there physically, he would always be with me. Those affirmations meant the world to me. My grandmother and I became much closer after Granddaddy passed. I later realized that because my grandfather and I were so close, my grandmother might have felt like she didn't have a chance to be as close with me. But we ended up developing a very close relationship that lasted into my adulthood.

Still, Granddaddy's death initiated a long phase in my life when I couldn't really celebrate Christmas. For 31 years, I was too scarred by what had happened to feel the joy of the holiday. It was not until my son was born in December of 2011 that Christmas acquired new meaning and hope for me.

***

My sister and my cousins and I dreaded returning to school after Christmas break. Our entire world had changed. How could we go back to our normal daily routines?

The first day back, our grief exploded into anger. On the bus, a younger boy who lived near us said to one of my cousins that he was glad our grandfather had died. I don't think he had any reason for saying it; I don't think he even knew Granddaddy. This kid had a track record of starting petty little fights with some of my cousins, and I think he was just being mean. But I'm pretty sure he regretted it, because a whole lot of Hamptons cousins pounced on him.

It was a big brawl, with all of us who were on the bus involved. The bus driver couldn't control it, so my grandmother had to get on the bus and pull each one of us off the kid, one by one. We were all suspended from the bus for three days for fighting. But I have to say, it was worth it. Even though we were heartbroken, my family and I were tighter than ever.

Life changed irreversibly after Granddaddy died, but it went on. In middle school, I tried out for the basketball team, and although I made the team, my pediatrician advised me not to play. Like my grandfather, my father, my sister, and several of my dad's siblings, I have genetic traits for sickle cell anemia, and the doctor said it could affect my oxygen levels. So I switched my focus to music. I sang in the chorus, and in sixth grade, I joined the band.

Playing instruments came naturally to me. By the seventh grade, I had learned to play the trombone, the flute, the saxophone, and the clarinet. Because I could play so many different instruments, I was asked to start playing with the high school marching band. First I played the flute because one of my cousins had one, but then I got braces, which made playing the flute painful. The band director switched me to the clarinet, but that hurt, too. Finally, he put me on the saxophone and trombone. I ended up shining on the trombone, so that's where I stayed.

When I finished middle school and went to high school, my parents made sure I stayed on the straight and narrow. Naturally, the teenage years bring new freedoms and new opportunities for trouble. An unplanned pregnancy for one of my good friends in the ninth grade really scared my parents, leading my dad to become very strict. Still, I was allowed some freedom. I was allowed to get my driver's license when I was 15, though it was restricted until I was 16. And because I was doing well in school, my parents even gave me a car—a gray 1991 Oldsmobile Cutlass that they had initially bought for themselves as their weekend car. Rolling up on campus in that car, I felt like I was driving a Bentley.

My parents did have a firm rule for when I drove: Only they, my sister, or my aunts and uncles were allowed to ride in my car. Not even my cousins were allowed to ride with me. My aunts and uncles adopted the same rule for all of my cousins when they got their driver's licenses.

One of my aunts worked in the cafeteria at my school, so we all knew she was keeping a sharp eye on us. Once, I learned how closely she was watching. One morning, I saw a female classmate whose car had broken down standing on the side of the road on the way to school. I wasn't going to leave her there, so I broke my parents' rule for the first time and picked her up. Of course, I didn't get away with it. My aunt saw me pull up to school with the girl. She pulled me out of class and asked what I was doing with someone in my car, because she knew my parents didn't allow it. I told Aunt Letha what happened, but that wasn't enough to get me off the hook. She pulled the girl out of class and listened to her confirmation of the story before she completely believed me.

But that was the closest I ever came to getting in trouble. Whether as a result of my parents' strict rules or just my own nature, I was a responsible, cautious teen. Every day I went to my part-time job at the local Piggly Wiggly after school, then home to do my homework. I didn't smoke or drink, and I still don't; in my circle of friends, I'm always the designated driver. All of my aunts and uncles were equally strict with my cousins, stemming from the way my grandparents raised their kids. From what I can surmise, it was a good method. None of us became a teen parent or was in the criminal justice system. In different ways, we have all gone on to thrive in our adult lives.

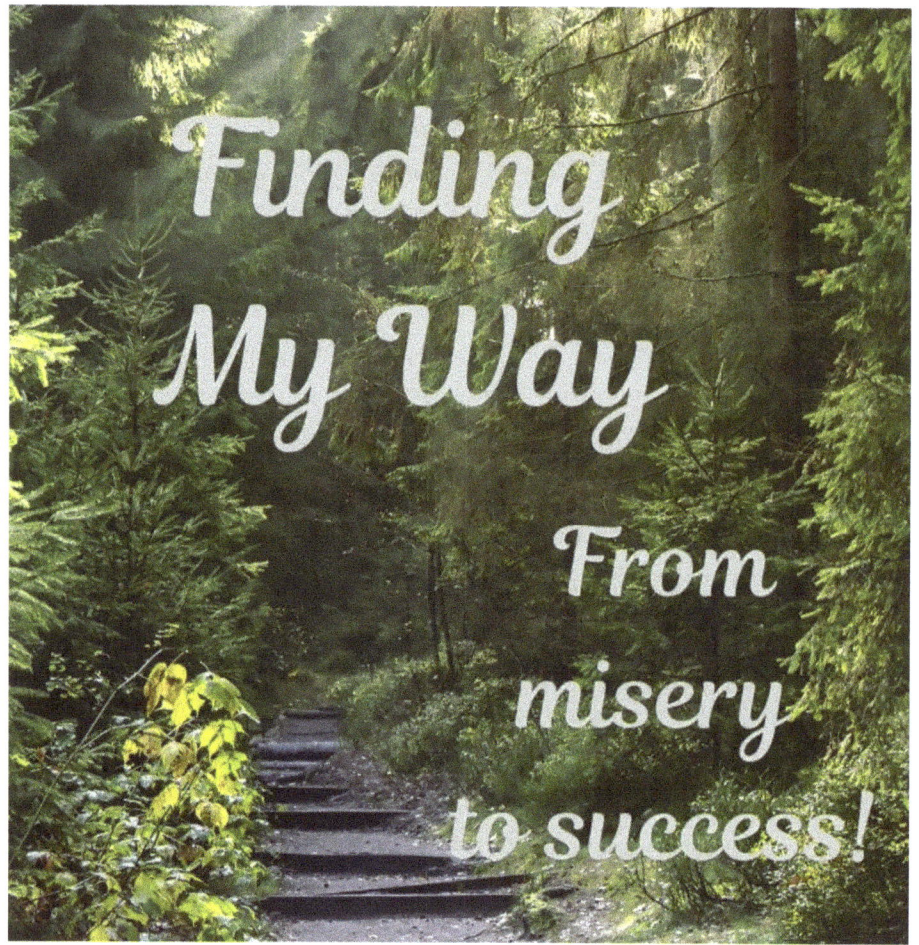

4

FINDING MY WAY (1995–2003)

As I neared the end of high school, I inevitably started to think about college. I was a good student, and I had a keen interest in computers, but I was wary of the debt that I knew I could accrue if I attended university straight after high school. Instead, I decided to join the Air Force.

There were two primary reasons for my decision. The first was the promise of a paid college education after service. I knew that I wanted to go to college, and not having to worry about student loans was a major incentive. But the more important reason I joined military was to honor my grandfather's legacy. Granddaddy had served in the Army, working as a cook during World War II. Although none of his children (my father's generation) had served, some of my male cousins had enlisted before me. However, none of the other granddaughters had done it, so I would be the first. Ultimately, the desire to honor Granddaddy was what drove me to enlist.

I was assigned to San Antonio for basic training. The flight I took from Columbia to Atlanta was my first time on an airplane. From there, I connected to a second flight from Atlanta to San Antonio. Going in, I was confident that I would be prepared. I had participated in a JROTC program in high school, so I was familiar with the structure I was walking into. I knew it wouldn't be easy, but I was ready.

As it turned out, my confidence was warranted. I thrived in the environment that others found grueling. We were required to wake up at 4 a.m. for physical training, but I was used to getting up early so I could pick vegetables from our gardens before it got too hot. My JROTC teachers had advised me to pace myself in physical training, because they said I would be expected to be faster every time, and that advice turned out to be spot-on. And the discipline from the drill sergeants was nothing compared to the way my parents ran our house.

However, being separated from my family wasn't quite so easy. I had never been away from them before, and that was harder than anything the drill sergeants could throw at me. The first time I called home, I hung up in tears. Then I called my grandmother, and hearing her voice just killed me. When the sound of a person's voice affects you that way, it truly demonstrates how much you love them.

As it turned out, my tenure in the Air Force didn't last long—but for a reason completely out of my control.

Upon enlisting, I had told the Air Force about my genetic trait for sickle cell anemia. I was told that it wouldn't be a problem. However, in the third week of basic training, the sergeant called me in to discuss it. He said the sickle cell traits could be problematic because I would be spending time at high elevations. I didn't have to leave, but if I were to get sick, the Air Force would offer no medical assistance.

Hearing that was devastating. Deep down, I knew the risk was too high to justify staying, but I wanted to fulfill my commitment and honor my grandfather. I called my grandmother to ask for her advice, and she told me that if she were me, she would come home. Her opinion was more important to me than anyone else's, so I listened.

Immediately upon arriving back in South Carolina, I started at Central Carolina Technical College. My parents had submitted my paperwork on my behalf. Our local church had granted me a scholarship of $500, which I used to buy my books. It wasn't the road I had set out on, but suddenly, I was a college student.

In my first semester, my dad convinced me to take a public speaking class. That class really challenged me. I don't consider myself a shy person, but generally, I would rather write a paper than give a speech, and that class took me out of my comfort zone. The hardest part was when we were required to give an impromptu speech. The professor would assign a random topic for each student to speak about for five minutes in front of the class. We couldn't research the topic beforehand, and we weren't allowed to say "um" or any other filler words. The whole ordeal was so anxiety-inducing that I couldn't sleep the night before.

Although I knew I'd never take another public speaking class, I wasn't sure what I wanted to study. I have always been fascinated by computers; one of the worst punishments of my life came after my parents bought me a word processor and took it apart (even though I put it back together and it still worked!). However, Central Carolina didn't offer a degree in computer science. I considering majoring in accounting, but when the initial classes didn't capture my interest, I knew it wasn't right for me.

Then one day at the college canteen, I started talking to a girl named Angela. One of her aunts had used to carpool with my grandmother in North Carolina. She was 10 years older than me, and she had gone back to school in the midst of a divorce, but despite being in different places in our lives, we soon found similarities in our ways of thinking and struck up a friendship. She became like a big sister to me, and we are still close friends today.

Angela was studying environmental engineering. After she told me about all the opportunities the degree afforded, I decided to try it, too. It turned out to be a good fit, and after two years, I received an associate's degree in environmental studies. Along the way, I started interning for the City of Sumter at the wastewater plant. Water would come through and then go to the water plant for treatment and consumption. My job was to collect water samples and take them to the lab to test for levels of fecal count, pH, sodium, and chlorine. After I'd completed my internship, I accepted a job there. I ended up working there for the rest of the time I attended Central Carolina.

The job was demanding; I worked 12-hour shifts, and I was scheduled every other weekend. It would have been difficult if I were married, but because I was a young student living with my parents, it worked well. The fact that my friend Angela worked there too made it more enjoyable for me. However, while I worked there, I quickly learned how challenging it can be for women working in a male-dominated environment. Our gender made some of the men think we didn't know what we were doing. Eventually, something happened that changed their mind.

The plant underwent some major renovations, adding water pumps so it could receive more water to be treated. After the new pumps were added, I noticed that a valve hadn't been installed correctly. When I turned it to close it, it continued to let more water in. I communicated the problem to the supervisor and told him they needed to get the construction crew in to fix it. I said that if it wasn't repaired immediately, the facility would flood within two hours. He ignored me and dismissed my advice, and sure enough, the plant flooded that night. Computers shorted, and testing equipment was destroyed by water damage. The flood cost the city $2 million.

That pretty much put an end to the sexism Angela and I had experienced. Our coworkers started to take our observations and assessments seriously in the plant, and we were even sent to represent the City of Sumter at conferences. It's unfortunate that it took that catastrophe for them to recognize our talent. In addition to costing the city a small fortune, it also slowed water distribution to the surrounding area for a while. Recently, the man who was working as the supervisor ran into my dad. He told him that not listening to me that day was his biggest regret.

After graduating with my associate's, I left my job at the plant and enrolled in St. Leo University, which was located at Shaw Air Force base in Sumter. I loved the 30-minute drive from my parents' house. I had bought a Chevrolet Blazer just after I'd finished my associate's degree, and I got a CD player with a changer in the trunk and set it up every morning with six CDs to play that day. However, going to classes on the base brought about mixed emotions for me. I was slightly envious of my classmates who were in uniform. They were living out the path I had expected to be on.

At St. Leo, I majored in computer science. I loved every aspect of my studies, but especially the potential for a high income. The only thing I didn't love was that I'd entered another male-dominated field. Often, I felt like I had to prove myself just to be taken seriously. I was keenly aware that the men in the room didn't have to do that. Every one of my professors was male, and one time, one of them told me condescendingly that I might be more valuable as a part of the university's nursing program. I answered firmly that I would be just as valuable, if not more, in the computer science program.

Apart from my studies, I worked two part-time jobs, one at Eckerd's and one at the South Carolina Waterfowl Association. For fun, I'd catch a movie or go bowling. And music was still a huge part of my life. I continued to sing in my church choir, and I played the trombone and the keyboard for fun. And I loved listening to music. My music taste is wide-ranging: I can go old-school or new-school. I'd listen to gospel music by Shirley Ceasar, Dottie Peoples, and Kirk Franklin; boy bands like NSYNC, New Kids on the Block, and Boyz II Men; Montell Jordan, Celine Dion, Escape, Sheila E., Prince, Michael Jackson, Gap Band, Commission, Fred Hammond—and the list goes on.

I graduated from St. Leo with a bachelor's degree in computer science and started a job with a local manufacturing company called Midwest Stamping. I worked as a computer technician and purchased supplies for the local plant. The job required frequent travel to the corporate headquarters in Toledo, Ohio. The company would fly me to Toledo to acquire knowledge from headquarters, and then upon my return, I would implement that knowledge and make sure the plant in Sumter was synchronized.

At the time, I was engaged to a man with whom I had been in a relationship for four years. However, he was unfaithful while I was traveling, and when I found out, I broke it off. A receptionist at my work named Joyce must have seen my heartbreak, because she asked me what was wrong, and I told her the whole story. Joyce suggested that I go on a date with her brother. She said he had been divorced for seven years, and he'd recently moved to South Carolina from New York City. I wasn't interested in being set up and I didn't want to date on a rebound, so I politely declined.

A few weeks later when Joyce invited me to a birthday party, I didn't suspect that her brother would be there. He didn't know I would be there, either. But thankfully, we did both attend, because her brother ended up being Jewel Jenkins.

My ♥
Belongs To My
Police Officer

5

A MAN NAMED JEWEL (1955–2003)

From my first conversation with Jewel at that party in February 2003, our connection was undeniable. We exchanged phone numbers, and soon we were talking on the phone every night for two or three hours. Jewel lived in Columbia, and I lived about an hour away in Sumter, so for a while, those phone calls comprised our relationship. Often, we'd talk so late that I would fall asleep while we were on the phone. Those were the days when people still used landlines, so he would call my parents' line to tell them to have me hang up.

After two or three weeks, we went out to dinner, and after that, we started eating dinner together every night. If we couldn't have dinner, we'd have lunch or breakfast. We were together constantly. Through February and March, we learned everything about each other.

Even though I was falling for Jewel, I was a little nervous for my family to meet him, mainly because he was 22 years older than me. I had always dated older men, but not that much older. I wasn't sure what my parents would think. However, once they got to know him and understood that his intentions were honorable, there wasn't a problem. In fact, a lot of my cousins ended up having large age gaps with their spouses, too.

One thing I didn't worry about was my family's perception of his race. Jewel was biracial: His mother was half Indian and half black, and his father was half black and half white. However, Jewel's skin was very light, so a lot of people saw him as a white man. In my family, we weren't raised to see color, and members of my generation have dated a wide variety of races and ethnicities, so he fit right in with my cousins. His career as a police officer gave him a point of connection as well, because most of my guy cousins also work in law enforcement.

When my family saw how naturally Jewel and I meshed, they assumed we had been dating for a lot longer than we had. They all got along so well with him. Everything was effortless. Honestly, it was as if God Himself had picked Jewel and me to be with each other.

One night that spring, Jewel presented me with a gift—a ring with a baby blue topaz stone.

"What's this?" I asked.

"It's a gift for you," he said.

"What does it mean?" I asked.

"It's a gift," he said.

I took him at his word, thinking he'd chosen it because he knew my signature colors are blue and purple. But three weeks later, he gave me a second ring—and this one came with a proposal. The topaz ring, he said, had been a placeholder.

In a way, I couldn't believe it. Our relationship had come about so quickly. Also, I had never imagined that I would marry a police officer, because I'd thought they were arrogant. But I prayed about his proposal, and I asked for my grandmother's advice. I tried hard to find a reason to say no, but all things said yes.

***

Jewel was born in Harlem on May 3rd, 1955. When I met him, I asked about his name, because I thought it sounded like a girl's name. He told me that when he was born, his mother looked at him and saw him as her jewel.

There were meanings behind the names of his siblings, too. Joyce, the sister who was born after him, who I'd met at Midwest Stamping, received her name because their mother felt she was going to bring her great joy. Their youngest sister, Faith, was born after their mother had a stroke that paralyzed her on her right side. Faith received her name because she was her mother's redemption child.

Jewel's mother, whose name was Lula Mae Harris Jenkins, had epilepsy. She was an independent-minded woman who never allowed her affliction to define her, but Jewel's father cared for her diligently, regularly cooking and cleaning for the family. He insisted on doing those jobs because he feared that his wife might have a seizure while she was cooking or cleaning and hurt herself. Jewel's father's name was Russell, but everyone—even his wife's father—called him "Mr. Jenkins."

Mr. Jenkins was from Virginia, but racial tensions had precipitated his move to New York. Jewel had a half-sister and half-brother from his previous marriage, as well as an older half-sister from his mother's previous marriage. He was very strict, with rules that the whole household had to comply with. He did not allow the family to have a phone in the house, and Jewel and his sisters had to be at home to eat dinner at 6 p.m. every evening. But he indulged them, too. He liked to take Jewel and his sisters out for clothes shopping trips. A driver named Big Al always escorted them in a Cadillac, and Mr. Jenkins told them to pick out whatever they wanted and always paid with cash. Jewel said those trips reminded him of the over-the-top shopping scene in *Pretty Woman*.

In later years, after he became a detective, Jewel questioned what his father did for work. Mr. Jenkins told the children that he worked at a brass foundry, but every day he went to work in a button-down white shirt, and those shirts were always professionally dry-cleaned and ironed. It didn't make sense that he would wear such formal attire to a job at a plant, where it was sure to get soiled.

Sadly, Jewel's father's true career remained a mystery, because he died of lung cancer in 1966, when Jewel was 11 years old. Jewel didn't attend the services, but his younger sisters did, and afterward, they told him about the staggering number of people who'd shown up. Later, Jewel regretted not attending, because he wondered if some of his questions might have been answered there.

After Mr. Jenkins died, Jewel's mother's father moved in with them and became kind of a surrogate father figure for Jewel and his sisters. The family could no longer afford the apartment they lived in, so they moved into public housing on the other side of Harlem. For Jewel, this caused severe culture shock. Because of the light color of his skin, he was bullied at the apartment complex as well as at his new school. But he turned that into motivation to get out of the housing projects. He was accepted into Chelsea Vocational Technical High School; then after graduation, he enrolled in John Jay College.

During the summers when he was in high school, Jewel's mother sent him to work at a camp in upstate New York. He said it was her way of getting him out of the hustle and bustle and stress of the housing projects and into nature. He had great memories from those summers. Two of his friends, Steve and Marty, would work alongside him, cleaning cabins and taking care of the campground, and on Fridays, after working all week, one of the guys would buy liquor and they would go to a cemetery and drink and play the Woodstock-era flower child music that Jewel always favored.

It didn't take long for Jewel to realize that college wasn't the right fit for him. He majored in computer programming, because building computers was a hobby of his, but he didn't want to work with computers as a profession. From the time he was young, his ambition was to become a police officer.

He had joined New York City's program for volunteer auxiliary police officers as soon as he turned 18, which was sort of like a glorified hall patrol or school safety patrol. The volunteers were only equipped with a scooter, no guns or other weapons, and their job was to maintain peace in their neighborhoods. But even though the position came with no pay and minimal power, Jewel delighted in his responsibilities.

In addition to being a volunteer police officer, Jewel worked part-time and helped care for his mother during college. Since he was her only son, he felt a particular duty to care for her the way his father had when he was alive. When Jewel turned 21, he left college and enrolled in the NYPD police academy, and the next year, in 1977, his mother passed away. In her absence, his aunt Ernestine (usually called Tina) and his grandfather's sister Maggie became the influential maternal women in his life.

After he graduated from the academy, Jewel was assigned to work with the NYPD's housing division. The housing division were the police for all of the apartment buildings throughout New York City. Often, their duties included going on roofs to break up drug activity or other crime.

Once, Jewel answered a call that led him onto the roof of a 17-story building. He saw the two perpetrators selling drugs, and he and his partner called out. The perps started to flee, and Jewel and his partner ran after them, but things took a turn for the worst when the man Jewel was chasing ran down a flight of stairs. It was not uncommon for people to urinate and defecate in the stairwells of those kinds of buildings, and that night, the stairs were covered in bodily fluids. Jewel slipped on the mess and went flying down the staircase.

When he told me this story years later, I had to laugh. At 5'7", my husband was a solid 240 pounds, so flying down those stairs, he must have been a sight. He was also a germaphobe, so I can only imagine the words that were coming out of his mouth as he slid downstairs covered in urine and fecal matter.

Eventually, the structure of the NYPD changed, and the different divisions of police were merged. At that point, Jewel became a police officer, and then later he was promoted to become a detective.

As a detective, Jewel worked in the aftermath of multiple bombings, including the first attack on the World Trade Center in 1993. He spent countless hours working New Year's Eve ceremonies at Times Square. He personally witnessed and investigated matters that the majority of the population would only know about by watching the news. I think he enjoyed that element of his job. Speaking about solving a crime or arresting a perp always gave his eyes an undeniable glow.

However, nothing in his career was as terrible or as infamous as what took place on September 11th, 2001.

***

September 11th happened to be Jewel's day off. That morning, he had gone to the house of the woman he was dating at the time in Englewood, New Jersey, and while he was there, he received a page from his captain. He called from the landline at her house and learned that two planes had flown into the Twin Towers of the World Trade Center.

By that point, chaos had already seized New York City. No one knew if more attacks were coming and where or when they might be. Jewel was told that he was needed at the precinct as soon as possible. In the wake of the attack, the entire NYPD was required to report to headquarters. But because he was in New Jersey, that was no easy feat. Traffic was so completely gridlocked that his drive from Englewood to Manhattan, normally a 40-minute trip, took five hours. After sitting in his car for a while on the New York side of the bridge, he realized nothing was going to move and got out of his car to walk the rest of the way, leaving his car parked on the side of the road.

Upon reporting to headquarters, Jewel was dispatched to one of the most gruesome epicenters of the devastation—

the morgue. When the towers had come down, many of the victims' bodies had been severed, leaving a huge number of disconnected body parts. At the morgue, the coroner was issuing death certificates as body parts were identified.

A few days later, Jewel was sent to the landfill in Staten Island. There, he and other officers sifted through loads of debris as they searched for identifiable body parts, wallets, or any type of identification. Immediately, Jewel started wearing a mask and protective gear. He knew that, in addition to being horrific, the task he'd been assigned was exposing him to dangerous toxins and could be incredibly harmful to his health. After the first 70-hour work week, he and his colleagues received respirators to use as they continued their work.

After three weeks at the landfill, Jewel was transferred back to the morgue, where death certificates were still being issued based on identifiable body parts. The goal was for families who were still missing loved ones to find closure. Without a death certificate, family members couldn't hold funerals or properly mourn the ones they'd lost, but the death certificates couldn't be issued until that identification was obtained. Some families had to wait for a death certificate for two or three years.

Jewel witnessed the coroner's communication to the families, and that experience caused him a great deal of mental anguish. Seeing the toll taken on the families was almost unbearable for him. It was tragic enough that their loved ones had been killed, but it made matters even worse that their bodies were often reduced to a mere body part—sometimes just an ear or half a finger. If it weren't for 9/11, Jewel probably would have stayed in New York. His entire life was there. But ultimately, the mental exhaustion affected him so entirely that he had to leave. In 2002, he decided to retire and move.

Jewel's two younger sisters had moved to Sumter, and he had visited them often. Despite being a born and bred New Yorker, he'd developed an affinity for the area. He wanted to be close to his sisters, but he also wanted to be in more of a city, so he decided to move to Columbia. He bought a house and settled in.

After he'd lived there for just over a year, he attended a birthday party his sister had invited him to. And that, of course, is where he met me.

cheers to love

6

HAPPY TOGETHER (2003–2011)

Jewel and I were married on June 29th, 2003, in a small ceremony held at my home church in Pinewood. I had never wanted a big wedding, so for me, it was perfect. Our wedding party consisted of my sister Kayla, two flower girls, and Jewel's oldest son.

Immediately, I loved and embraced Jewel's sons from his two previous marriages. From the beginning, I've seen them as my "bonus sons," and as time goes on, my relationships with them continue to grow. Now that I also have Jace, I tell people I have three boys.

Jewel Bobby is the older of the bonus sons, born during Jewel's first marriage on January 14th, 1984. His father's namesake, he is very much the protector of the two brothers, and he continually strives to please my late husband. He has two children, and he's engaged to be married. He loves cars, which got him into some trouble when he was a teenager. He got in the habit of speeding and racing, thinking that since his dad was a cop, he'd never get in too much trouble.

Finally, Jewel pushed back. One time when Jewel Bobby was pulled over for speeding, Jewel told the officer to lock him up in jail for an hour. That scared him badly enough to stop him from racing again.

Jewel's second son is Kristopfer Matthew, born on May 15th, 1993. He and Jewel Bobby work together as medical carriers for Northwell. They drive all over New York City and New Jersey, picking up and delivering medical specimens. They go in to work together at 4 p.m. and work until midnight. They know that I worry about them, and I know they worry about me, so every day, they call me when they wake up in the morning, when they arrive at the hospital for work, and when they get home at night. They talk to Jace every day, too. The three of them have always had a very close bond, but since Jewel passed, their bond has become even stronger.

After the wedding, Jewel and I went to Montreal for a week for our honeymoon, and when we returned, I moved into his house in Columbia. For the first few years, we traveled extensively and lived spontaneously. We never stopped dating or having fun together. We indulged our shared love of computers by going to computer shows together and buying new parts so he could continue to build faster computers for us.

Jewel was fastidious in maintaining the cleanliness of our house, our car, our yard, and all of his other belongings. At his funeral, one of his friends from the police department remarked that when he came over to our house for dinner, the floors were as squeaky clean as the floors in a bowling alley. That perfectionism was reflected in our relationship, too. He took great pains to make sure I was cared for, cooking and cleaning for me the way his father had done for his mother, even though I wasn't restricted by a long-term illness the way she was.

In the beginning of our marriage, I noticed that he became tense and closed off any time the subject of 9/11 arose. He had witnessed an overwhelming amount of grief, and I don't think he had been able to process it yet. Jewel always wanted to fix things and make them right, so I think seeing the physical and emotional devastation caused by the attack and not being able to carry out action that would directly bring justice to the terrorists who had done it made him feel helpless. He felt that, as a police officer, he should have been able to do more for the families he saw grieving.

Seeing the way it had all impacted him, I suggested that he go to therapy. He agreed, but he told me the therapists he saw didn't understand. My opinion was that as long as he was talking to someone about it, he would make progress, and it proved to be true. Eventually, I saw the tension ease as he relaxed into himself. It was difficult to navigate as a newly married couple, but I'm glad that I got to be a part of that healing process for him. I met him at his lowest point, so I was able to appreciate him there and value him even more when he reached his highest.

Although Jewel had retired from the NYPD, after moving to Columbia in 2002 and living the retired life for a while, he realized he was bored. He decided to go back to work and joined the Richland County police force in Columbia. He was happy to be working again, but he encountered a lot of bigotry—mostly because he was from the north. The force was run differently from what he was used to. In the north, the two officers always rode together in a patrol car, but that wasn't the case in the south. Even though he had worked as a detective for 20 years, in Richland County, where he was a deputy, his colleagues often pushed back on his suggestions.

Jewel moved to the civil process division, which handled evictions and foreclosures for the courts. It was a nine-to-five job, which was ideal for me, since we had just gotten married, but he felt he wasn't being respected for his expertise as a patrolman. I could see in his eyes that it wasn't enjoyable for him: he missed the thrill of the action.

After that, he joined the Columba police department. On the first call that he went out on, he found three dead bodies in a canal near an apartment complex. At 4 a.m., he called me to tell me that he was OK, because he knew I was going to see the story on the news in the morning. Sure enough, when I woke up, I saw the report on the local news and found out that he was the first officer on the scene.

There were some funny incidents during his time with the Columbia PD, too. Before moving to South Carolina, he had never seen ant mounds. One day he went on a call and while he and the backup deputy were talking to the homeowner in the backyard, he didn't realize that he had stepped into a fire ant mound. In the police academy, he'd been taught to rock from side to side if he was in an untidy house to keep the roaches away, so he tried that tactic, but it didn't work. The ants were crawling inside his pant legs and biting him all over.

Panicking, Jewel started peeling off his pants. At this point, his legs were covered in fire ants. There was a lake nearby, and the backup deputy told him to jump in the water. He stripped down to his boxers, beelined to the lake, and jumped in. After that, the homeowner they'd been talking to kept calling the station and asking for him. Apparently, when he'd stripped down, he'd made her so hot and bothered that she couldn't stop thinking about him. I laughed and laughed when I heard that story, and I'd bring it up every time we saw a fire ant mound.

But generally, it seemed he was always assigned to urban areas where the crime was getting progressively worse. When he worked in those areas in the middle of the night, I worried that the light color of his skin essentially marked him with a bullseye. Ultimately, he left when the police department implemented profiling patrolling. If the officers saw Black or Hispanic people out walking at night, they were supposed to stop and ask them for identification. Jewel didn't think that was fair, and he also didn't want someone to sue him.

Fortunately, around that time, a position became available with the Bureau of Protective Services, which provides security for state buildings, the governor's mansion, and the state capitol as well as security detail for the governor. They reached out to him, and he decided to pursue the opportunity.

The application process was strenuous, because they had to dig into not only Jewel's background, but also mine. They came to visit us at home and interviewed me to make sure I was on board with him working in this capacity and that I understood that his work hours might fall outside of the norm. Since we didn't have children yet, I agreed. On the weekends when he had to work, I would go to get my hair done on Saturday mornings, and on weekends when he didn't have to work, we relished the time together.

Jewel built great relationships in that job. Nikki Haley, who was the governor when he retired, is now Jace's godmother, and her husband is his godfather. I am still cordial with Mark Sanford, who was the governor from 2003 to 2011 and who went missing for several days while he was in office. Eventually it was discovered that he was not actually missing but had absconded to Argentina to be with his mistress. I am also still cordial with the wife, who ended up divorcing him. Although Jewel never worked with the current governor, Henry McMaster, he and his wife came to our house, and we adopted two cats from them.

My career took a few turns during those years, too. As soon as Jewel and I had returned from our honeymoon, the company I'd been working for, Midwest Stamping, told me that I'd been transferred to the corporate office in Toledo, Ohio. I was frustrated, because my superiors there knew I had just gotten married, and neither Jewel nor I wanted to move to Ohio. So I left my job. The timing ended up being fortuitous, because Jewel's son Kristopfer was coming for the summer. It was the perfect time for me to stay home and spend quality time with him.

After that, I worked in the IT department of the Board of Education for two years, and then I worked at a local law firm, first in IT and then in legal IT. But several years later, my husband's aunt Tina, who'd stepped in to be an important maternal figure for him after his mother passed away, became very sick and was placed on life support. With her medical needs, we weren't able to move her from New York to South Carolina, but Jewel wanted to be there for her, so we moved to New Jersey for a while. We got an apartment in Belleville, New Jersey, and I took a job there with a legal discovery company. My job was to do IT-style forensics for different law firms and find things on hard drives that people thought they'd hidden. Jewel was still working for the BPS, so he traveled to South Carolina every other week for work.

Jewel was a Yankee to the core. Even after acquiring a slight Southern drawl, a pickup truck, and a more Southern way of thinking, he always identified as a New Yorker. He sounded like a New Yorker, too—especially if he was upset about something. Whenever we visited the city, which was often during those years, his favorite thing to do was eat. Some of his favorite cuisines, like Russian, Italian, and different types of Chinese, weren't readily available in South Carolina, so he would eat as much of his favorite foods as he could. Still, he never wanted to move back permanently. In New York City, he had lost both of his parents, seen the failures of two marriages, and experienced 9/11 and all the trauma that came in the aftermath.

Although I was happy to be there to help and support his aunt, I had no real desire to live in New Jersey, either. I have sort of a love/hate relationship with the north. When Aunt Tina eventually passed, we no longer had a reason to be there, so we relocated back down south.

Upon our return to Columbia in 2010, there were no openings at the law firm where I had been working. Instead, I started teaching at Centaura College. I taught two classes in the mornings and two classes in the evenings, including classes on computer programming, servers, Microsoft Office, and computer hardware.

Jewel and I were blissfully happy in our marriage for those years. Still, there was something missing. Struggles with infertility were getting in the way of our desire to have children. For years, I had been afflicted by uterine fibroids. I had undergone surgery to remove some of them, but not all of them were able to be removed. As a result, three different doctors had told me that I might not be able to have children.

I have always been a private person, slow to share my troubles. By nature, I don't like to rely on people. There have been times in the past when I have relied on people and it's been used against me. In response, I built a quiet strength and resilience that allows me to push through situations, regardless of how difficult they are. That's how I handled the infertility issue. My condition with the fibroids and my disappointment about what the doctors had told me remained my private burdens, with only Jewel aware of the extent of the situation.

What made those years especially hard was that I didn't understand *why* it was happening. Jewel and I had joined a Baptist church together. He had grown up Baptist, and although I was Methodist, the denominations were similar enough, and it was important for us to join a church together as a married couple. So I was still an active, churchgoing Christian, and I wanted to have a child with my husband. When years passed without me becoming pregnant, I couldn't help blaming myself and wondering if it was somehow my fault. I didn't understand why God would withhold this from me, just like I didn't understand why He had taken my grandfather from me.

Jewel loved me and supported me through it all. He just kept saying that if it was meant to be, it would be. I knew that he wanted to have a child with me, but he insisted that his love for me would never change, whether I was able to get pregnant or not.

ALONG CAME this LITTLE MIRACLE and no DAY was EVER ORDINARY AGAIN.

7

JACE (2011–2017)

During my years of infertility, my grandmother was constantly asking when I was going to have a baby. I never told her about my struggles with the fibroids; I just said Jewel and I were enjoying our life together and that we were content having my two bonus sons. But my grandmother wasn't buying it. One day, she said that until she saw me have a child or become pregnant, she wasn't going anywhere. I laughed it off, because I thought there was no way that was going to happen, but she ended up having the last laugh.

Grandmother passed away on the morning of Tuesday, April 11th, 2011. Three days later, on April 14th, it occurred to me that I hadn't had my cycle. I was running around getting things organized for her funeral, and while I was in CVS printing some photos, I bought a pregnancy test. I took the test, and it was positive. Then I took about seven more, and all of them were positive. Instantly, I remember what my grandmother had said, and I knew that when she had left this earth, she had made a way for my child to enter.

Because I had been told that I probably couldn't get pregnant, I was afraid to share the news, so Jewel and I decided not to tell anyone for a while. It was a decision we made out of fear, in an effort to protect our emotions as well as everyone else's.

Soon after that, I became extremely sick. I knew that some sickness was normal for the beginning of a pregnancy, and I also chalked it up to stress from my grandmother's death. My sister was planning her wedding, and she asked me to go dress shopping with her, and even though I was so sick, there was no way I was going to say no to her. However, because I was feeling so ill, I was kind of trying to rush through the appointment. She noticed and asked what was wrong, and I told her I wasn't feeling well, but she knew I was hiding something. Finally, I had to tell her. She was beyond excited, and she started shopping for the baby immediately.

As my pregnancy progressed, I kept getting sicker. I could barely keep any food down. I didn't tell anyone how sick I was, though. I was determined to handle it privately, the way I handled everything else. But eventually, I couldn't hide what I was going through from the people closest to me.

At my six-week checkup, seeing that I had lost weight and was combating terrible sickness, the doctor put me on modified bedrest, instructing me to limit my working day to no more than six hours. In June, at my three-month appointment, I had lost so much weight and become so dehydrated that the doctor put me in a wheelchair and sent me directly to the hospital. My parents found out what was going on when my mother called to ask how the appointment had gone and she heard the nurse talking about inserting the IV through the phone.

From that point on, I was on bedrest for the rest of my pregnancy. I had an IV and a Zofran pump, which Jewel changed the catheter for every night. He doted on me throughout the pregnancy. He never missed an OB appointment. He took me out for rides in the car whenever he wasn't working and brought home my favorite foods from my favorite restaurants, even though I couldn't keep anything down. He tried every remedy you could think of to help me. Still, I kept losing weight. Over the course of the pregnancy, I lost 40 pounds.

I also started having severe back pain, and an ultrasound showed that I had gallstones. They can only be removed by removing your gallbladder, and I couldn't have that done while I was pregnant, so I had to wait it out. The problem ended up intensifying after the birth, and I had the procedure in 2013. Before that, I was an emotional eater, so I would often turn to junk food like honey buns and potato chips when I was under stress, but since then, I've adopted healthier eating habits.

Coincidentally, the only week I wasn't sick came at the perfect time. Jewel and I had booked a vacation for July—a cruise that would go to Grand Turk, Nassau, and Half Moon Cay. My doctor was leery of me going because my sickness had been so extreme. She insisted on talking to the cruise line and the doctor who would be onboard and filling them in on my situation. Eventually, she signed off on it, and that week turned out to be the best I felt the entire pregnancy.

Being on bedrest was a struggle mentally as well as physically. I entertained myself with crossword puzzles and my phone, but it was hard being idle when I was used to working. I ended up taking a leave from work under the Family and Medical Leave Act, but it was unpaid, so I had no income. I had some money saved, but you can't keep spending without replenishing, and with a new baby on the way, there was a lot we needed to buy.

However, my family threw us a big baby shower. Then our church did one, and our community that we were living in did a third one for us. Between the three baby showers, we were given everything a baby could need and more. It was beautiful to see so much support from the people around me.

But Jewel and I still had more to figure out financially. When we calculated how much it would cost to put our child in daycare, we realized the numbers didn't make sense. My entire paycheck would have gone to childcare. One day, Jewel called me and said that he was eligible for retirement and that he was ready to hang his hat up. He'd never had the opportunity to be with his older two sons when they were infants, and he wanted to stay home and take care of our child.

Jewel and I discussed it, and then I discussed it with my parents and my sister. He'd never cared for an infant before, and I didn't know how he was going to do it. But finally I thought, "What's the worst that could happen?" I agreed. Jewel stopped working on October 1st, 2011, and then officially retired and became a full-time stay-at-home dad on January 1st, 2012.

***

The nine months of my pregnancy were excruciating, but I finally made it to the end. Because of my preexisting condition with the fibroids, my only option was to have a C-section. It was scheduled for December 14th, when I was 39 weeks pregnant.

Going into the surgery, my anxiety was high. Jewel and I both anticipated potential complications. Before the birth, the doctor had predicted that the baby would weigh about six pounds. In the midst of the C-section, I heard my baby boy cry, which was music to my ears—but then a burst of panic followed when the doctor said, "Oh my God."

Jewel and I were both alarmed, to say the least. Thankfully, it turned out that nothing was wrong—the doctor was simply in shock because the baby was eight pounds and 13 ounces. We named our baby boy Jace. I had heard the name on a TV show called *Teen Moms,* and I thought it was both beautiful and a name that would serve him well as he grew up and went into the workplace. Jace was absolutely perfect, with no health issues whatsoever.

I was ecstatic that I had come out the other side with no complications and a beautiful, healthy baby, and I was also excited that I would now be able to eat! Only one person could join me in the recovery room, so my mother came and spent some time with me. I was feeling a little queasy, so I was nervous to eat, but I drank some tea and attempted to eat some applesauce. Immediately, everything came back up.

Between the exhaustion, the hormones, and the roller coaster of emotions I'd just experienced, it felt like the last straw. I started bawling uncontrollably. I was so tired of vomiting, and all I wanted to do was eat. Would I ever be able to eat normally again? Once I'd calmed down, the doctor told me that my stomach was probably just upset because of the anesthesia. Thankfully, that turned out to be correct. Soon, I was able to eat like I had before I was pregnant, with no nausea. It was such a relief to be able to enjoy food again. I remember my first big meal post-birth—a cheeseburger and fries with a sweet tea.

***

Since Jace was born on December 14th, he was a brand-new infant that Christmas of 2011. For the first time since my grandfather had died, I felt like I had a reason to celebrate Christmas again. Since I'd had a C-section less than two weeks before, I wanted to keep it low-key, but Jewel didn't do anything low-key.

He let me sleep in Christmas morning, and when I came downstairs, he and Jace were sitting at the Christmas tree waiting for me, and it looked like a Toys R Us explosion in our living room. Obviously, Jace was far too young to recognize what was going on, but Jewel was determined to celebrate Christmas at full intensity.

Then I went into our other living room and saw that he had set up a second tree. This one, he said, was my tree. He had bought me clothes, jewelry, and everything else that he knew I liked. "What in the world?" I said.

"Thank you," he said. "Thank you for giving me my son. Thank you for being you."

I was crying, of course. I couldn't believe it. But that was Jewel. He always went the extra mile to make sure everyone in his circle felt loved. From then on, we made the decision that even though Jace's birthday is very close to Christmas, he would always have two separate celebrations.

Since I was still recovering, my parents came to our house later that day, and they brought gifts, too. It was a low-key celebration, but we ate and spent time together, and my parents doted on Jace. Since my parents had two daughters, Jace is like the son they never had, and they adore him.

I'll never forget the first time my sister met Jace. Kayla had never been around a small child before, and seeing how she doted on him and loved him could move anyone to tears. She and her husband, Michael, had their wedding in September of 2012. I was the matron of honor, and Jace, at nine months old, wore a tiny tux. On November 27th, 2013, Kayla and Michael had their own child, a girl named Layla. Just like Kayla and me, she and Jace are the best of friends.

***

Jewel immediately embraced his role as Jace's dad. While I recovered, he jumped into diaper duty and formula duty. Jace had a huge appetite as a baby, so he drank an unbelievable amount of formula. He'd drink 10 bottles a day, which amounted to a quart! The local BiLo started ordering cases of formula just for us, so they never even hit the shelf.

After my maternity leave, I returned to Centaura College, but I gave up my night classes and only taught during the day. Two months after my return, a law firm in Charlotte, North Carolina, reached out and made me an offer I couldn't pass up. I only hesitated because the drive to Charlotte was an hour and 15 minutes, but Jewel encouraged me to take it. He had a way of making me feel like a million dollars even when I didn't see my own value. When I doubted my abilities, he would tell me to go for it.

After I accepted the job, I excelled and worked my way up the ranks. I did that commute for a year and a half, and then, in August of 2013, we moved into a house that we had built in Charlotte. Later, I was contacted by Securitas, a company that handles the security cameras for the branches and the ATMs of Bank of America and Wells Fargo. They offered me an even better package, so I started working there and remained there until I officially retired in August of last year.

Every evening when I came home from work, Jewel would have bathed Jace, and then he would go to the gym and run errands so I could have special bonding time with the baby, feeding him and putting him down to sleep. Often, he would come home with clothes for Jace and me from Kohl's or JC Penney.

Having worked 9/11 and experienced terrorism firsthand, Jewel was hyper-aware and extremely protective. He would scope out every area we entered, searching for potential dangers like he was a bodyguard. Once Jace was born, those protective tendencies heightened. Every two hours in the night, he would get up and look out the windows and at the security cameras.

But he was also the most amazing, fun, gentle stay-at-home dad. He loved to take Jace out and about to the park or the playground, the pool, the mall, the movies, or car lots. (Jewel was a car enthusiast, which is why Jace now has a love of sports cars.) He'd take him to do the grocery shopping, the bank, and to doctors' appointments. And at least once a week, they would meet me for lunch. People in our community always gushed to me about what a perfect dad Jewel was, and I had to agree.

Jewel also took Jace to different state posts in South Carolina where he'd worked. Officers who work there still contact me, ask about Jace, and send him things. That's strange for me, because, as a giver myself, it can be difficult for me to accept gifts. I have to remind myself that those gifts signify the impact Jewel made on them. I think it speaks volumes about the power of his influence that, two years after his passing, people still go out of their way to show that they think of him fondly.

8

BATTLING CANCER (2017–2020)

Jewel's mother had both breast cancer and leukemia, and his father died of lung cancer. Because of his family history with cancer, he was particularly health-conscious. He worked out regularly, drank protein shakes, and went to the doctor for regular checkups. In April of 2017, at one of those regular checkups, he asked the doctor about a lump he had discovered on his wrist.

The doctor was unconcerned. He said it was probably either a cyst or a work-related injury. They took an X-ray, but the scan didn't show any abnormality, so the doctor said they would look at it again at his appointment in September.

By September, the lump had grown significantly. At that appointment, the doctor sent him to get an MRI over Labor Day weekend. That weekend, we happened to be holding a retirement cookout for my mom. Not wanting to disrupt the festivities, Jewel told me that the doctor had sent him to see a specialist, but he didn't tell me that the specialist was an oncologist.

I took an early lunch to go to the appointment with him. The hospital was across the street from my office, so Jewel came and picked me up. In that appointment, Jewel was diagnosed with stage four non-Hodgkin lymphoma. Ironically, the date of the appointment was September 11th, 2017—exactly 16 years after the attack that had changed his life and exposed him to terrible toxins.

Hearing the news, both Jewel and I were in shock. He had always been the healthy one; I was the one who'd dealt with health challenges. But the doctor assured us that the news wasn't as bad as it might sound.

"If you're going to get cancer," he said, "this is the one you want to get."

He explained that in this case, having stage four cancer was actually a good thing. The higher the stage, he said, the better the response to treatment. Although I'm grateful that he gave us a positive outlook on the situation, they gave me no indication of the battle we were walking into.

***

The doctor had told us that Jewel's cancer would be treated with six chemotherapy treatments. Before they could begin, Jewel had to undergo a plethora of tests—biopsies, tests on his heart, a fitting for a line they would place under the skin for the chemotherapy to be administered. For two weeks, we went to appointments every day.

Still, Jewel moved along like nothing had changed. To see him go through his daily life, you would never guess that anything was wrong. I was breaking down but trying hard not to let it show. To appease my anxious mind, I learned as much as I could about Jewel's condition. I researched extensively and joined every forum I could find on Facebook. This helped me understand medical lingo when we met with doctors, which allowed me to defuse Jewel when he felt uneasy.

Once the chemotherapy commenced, Jewel went in for a treatment on a Tuesday every three weeks. After we saw the doctor, he would be hooked up to the IV at the chemo station to receive five different IV bags, plus steroids. There were 30 little pods in that area of the hospital, and each one had a recliner with a TV and a DVD player. But rather than sitting and relaxing, Jewel would always opt to socialize. He would go from pod to pod and encourage the other patients getting treatment. Sometimes he would bump into someone who would ask if he was from New York, and they'd get into a conversation, and the next thing you knew, his machine was beeping because the treatment was over. He was a true social butterfly who never met a stranger, and he inspired everyone to hang in there.

There was one man we saw receiving chemo a few times before Jewel talked to him. This man looked very frail and feather-light, and he was always wheeled in a wheelchair. One day Jewel went up and talked to him, and the man told him that he was on his 60th chemo treatment. He told Jewel that he wasn't giving up. He said he knew he didn't look good, but he was still fighting. For once, Jewel was the one who was inspired. I remember he said, "I guess I don't have an excuse."

Jewel's body responded remarkably well to the treatments. He never threw up or suffered any side effects from the chemo. He even pressure-washed our neighbors' driveway when they were in Ethiopia for a month. They hadn't asked him to do it, but it was his nature to help, and he still had so much strength and energy.

After three of the six treatments, a PET scan determined that the cancer was gone. When we found out, we started celebrating. We couldn't wait for the next doctor's appointment, because we assumed he would say Jewel didn't need the other three treatments. However, the doctor said that he would still need to complete the last three treatments. Non-Hodgkin's lymphoma is a blood cancer, which provides less of a warning than organ cancers, so they wanted to make sure it was gone.

In January of 2018, Jewel finished the chemo. Jewel Bobby's birthday is close to mine, so we always celebrated our birthdays together in January. That year, the celebration was extra special because we were also celebrating Jewel being done with chemo.

However, the doctor had informed us that they also were going to administer 17 rounds of radiation to ensure that all the cancer was gone. For those treatments, Jewel went in five days a week for three weeks and two days. When that was completed, the scans showed that he was still in remission. We were confident that his battle with cancer was over.

But a few months later, shortly after we celebrated Jewel's 53rd birthday in May, the rug was pulled out from under us when we learned that the cancer had returned.

That was the first of many terrible disappointments. Every time he relapsed, our hopes were crushed. The roller coaster effect was excruciating for me, and seeing him go through it was even more painful. Eventually, we stopped celebrating remissions. We never knew how long a remission would last, and we didn't want to set ourselves up for the inevitable pain when our hopes were extinguished.

***

The next treatment Jewel underwent was called R-DHAP. He was able to receive some of the treatment as an outpatient, but for other parts of it, he had to be admitted to the hospital for two days at a time so the doctor could monitor any repercussions of the powerful chemotherapy. He received three treatments of that, which prepared his body for a stem cell transplant, which is also called a bone marrow transplant. He was admitted to the hospital for the stem cell transplant just after Thanksgiving of 2018.

The transplant required him to stay in the hospital for 30 days while the doctors waited for the cells to start responding. Throughout that month, I went to see him every day on my lunch break. He remained upbeat and social. One lunch break when I went to visit him, he wasn't in his room. When

I called him, I heard his phone ringing in a different room. I found him in there playing checkers with a patient who was about to start his treatment. In spite of what he was going through, he spread good cheer throughout that ward.

Jace and I video called him every morning and evening, but Jace didn't know he was in the hospital. We had told him that Poppy (Jace's name for Jewel) was at the police academy. It was a valid lie, since Jewel was still officially with the South Carolina police at that point, and we did it with the best intentions for our son.

We tried our best to shield him from the reality of his dad's disease. He knew that Poppy had cancer; toward the beginning, he had noticed that I wasn't going to work at the normal time, which was because I was attending all of Jewel's appointments and treatments, and he knew something had changed. We told him that Poppy had something in his blood called cancer but that we were getting medicine in his blood to get the cancer out.

Even though we did our best to protect him from the seriousness of the situation, we couldn't hide it entirely. Seeing all the appointments written on the calendar at our house made him worry, so Jewel and I stopped writing them on that calendar and kept track of the appointments in the calendars on our phones. That December, while he was in the hospital for the stem cell transplant, Jewel missed Jace's birthday party for the first time.

For a while, the stem cell transplant seemed to have worked. In January of 2019, Jewel was in remission again. However, his immune system had been reduced to that of a newborn baby. He needed to get inoculations all over again to protect him from common diseases, but he wasn't strong enough to do that yet, so he could no longer go to places with crowds, and any time he was out in public, he had to wear a mask. Those were the days before the pandemic, when no one wore masks, and he was self-conscious about it. Rather than drawing attention to himself, he opted to stay in or go out only early in the mornings.

Then, in April, the cancer was back. This time, the doctors told us about a new treatment called a CAR T-cell treatment. It required them to remove cells from Jewel's body, attach a chemo-type medicine, and then put them back for the chemo to fight the cancer internally. It was an incredibly expensive procedure, to the tune of $500,000. We had to get a number of insurance approvals, but that wasn't a problem. Jewel's recovery was our only concern, and we were willing to do what we had to do to achieve it.

Jewel received the CAR T-cell treatment in June and was in remission within days. However, it affected his platelets and his hemoglobin so that he became transfusion-dependent. Every other week or so, he would have to go into the hospital to get a transfusion of platelets and hemoglobin. The scary part about that was that if the cancer were to return, he wouldn't be able to receive any other cancer treatment because his body wouldn't be strong enough.

***

In January of 2020, Jewel felt a lump in his leg. He told the doctors, but they didn't seem to take it seriously, and his transfusions continued. But in February of 2020, scans showed that the cancer had returned once again.

This time, we were advised to try a Hail Mary treatment to attempt to slow the cancer down. It was a low level of chemotherapy, designed for lung cancer. Unfortunately, that strategy ended up backfiring. The lymphoma combated the chemotherapy with growth, and new lymphoma masses started appearing everywhere—on his back, on his face. His legs swelled because fluid that would normally drain out was blocked. The internal masses were blocking his body's lymphatic system.

Our next step was a trip to New York City to see a specialist at Sloane Kettering, but they didn't have anything to offer us. That was in early March of 2020, right around the time that COVID-19 hit. The pandemic changed the world, but for us, it was sidelined by the health crisis we had already been dealing with. He'd been wearing masks and avoiding large groups of people ever since his bone marrow transplant. It was like the world had just caught up.

At that point, Jewel received some information that I didn't learn about until later. When I was in the bathroom during the appointment, the doctor told him that he had reached the end of the road in terms of treatments they could try and that the best that they could offer was hospice. When I returned from the bathroom, neither Jewel nor the doctor filled me in, so I didn't know how dire the situation was. For his part, Jewel didn't accept the doctor's prognosis. He was determined to keep fighting.

We learned about an option that could potentially help Jewel at Duke University Medical Center, so we road tripped there for an appointment on May 6th, 2020. However, now that COVID-19 was in full swing, everything was more complicated. I wasn't allowed to go inside, so I listened in on the appointment from my phone in the car. The doctors at Duke said that Jewel was a candidate for the treatment, but that before they could begin it, they would have to get authorization.

After that appointment, we were both optimistic. Still positive and gregarious, Jewel was calling friends and acquaintances who had been diagnosed with COVID-19 and encouraging them. But with everyone working at home because of the pandemic, the necessary authorization proved to be hard to obtain. As each day passed without good news, Jewel's mental determination remained as strong as ever, but his body grew progressively weaker.

9

SAYING GOODBYE (2020)

By May of 2020, Jewel's legs had become so swollen by the tumors blocking his lymphatic system that he could no longer walk. Physically, he depended on me for everything. I was more than happy to care for him: He was my husband, who I adored, and he had cared for me so selflessly during my turbulent pregnancy. But I know that for him, it was bone-crushing for me to have to care for him like that.

One Sunday, he told me he had to go to the bathroom. I wheeled his chair to the bathroom, and he tried to urinate, but couldn't. When I got him back into his chair, he told me he needed to go to the emergency room. I offered to drive him, but he didn't want Jace to have to come with us, so he wanted to call an ambulance. He had me add credits to Jace's account for his favorite video game, then called Jace downstairs to tell him. Jace was so excited, and he ran upstairs to play. Only then, after Jace was distracted, did Jewel let me call the ambulance.

As we waited for it to arrive, he looked at me and said, "Reese, I'm just tired." At that moment, I saw something in him that I hadn't seen before. As I watched him leave, I had a premonition that things were going to go downhill from there.

***

The doctor called to tell me they were going to admit Jewel because of the severe swelling in his legs. They gave him morphine to help with the pain and planned to meet with his team to determine the next steps. The next day, Jewel called me and said the doctors wanted to talk to both of us on a video call. On that call, the doctor told us that the cancer was beyond the point of return. Jewel's only option was hospice.

I was at a loss for words. How was I going to do this? I couldn't imagine calling everyone who should know or figuring out what to tell Jace. No one would be prepared. Like me, Jewel is a private person, so he had shared very little about his cancer battle with our family and friends. It was not until after he had passed that people in our lives understood the number and the intensity of the treatments he had undergone.

Even though I felt paralyzed with shock, I knew that we had to act. The doctor had said that Jewel could spend his final days in a facility or at home, and Jewel wanted to come home. First, I needed to talk to Jace. I sat him down and told him that Poppy might go to heaven soon. I said that he was going to come home, and he might still get better at the house, but if he went to heaven, he would be able to watch over us and protect us.

We also told Jewel Bobby and Kristopfer, and after that, we told my parents, my sister, and his sisters. As soon as Jewel Bobby and Kristopfer heard the news, they started driving from New York. They got in Thursday at 1 p.m., and Jewel arrived home from the hospital that same day at 3 p.m.

Even then, Jewel was his normal vivacious, jubilant, outgoing self, with a big appetite and a bigger personality. He joked around, talked to friends on the phone, and ate and drank everything in sight. There was no show of pain or labored breathing. He was still 240 pounds, and he ate like crazy, requesting Frosties from Wendy's and frankfurters from Sonic. None of us could quite believe that his time on earth was limited.

Three days after he'd arrived home, on the morning of Sunday, May 24th, Jewel grabbed me and pulled me in to him. He said, "I just want to thank you. You didn't have to stay by my side."

"Yes, I did," I answered. "Those vows are serious."

"Well, I picked a good one," he said.

Then he asked if I could fix him some grits. He always loved my grits.

I went to the kitchen and cooked his grits, and when I was walking down the hall to bring them to him, I thought I heard him say my name. I can't say for sure if he really said it or not, but I do know that when I turned the corner, I saw a glow over him that was almost angelic. Immediately, I knew that he was gone.

I went to him and checked his pulse, and there was nothing. Jewel had flown away.

***

Everything in me wanted to start CPR, but Jewel had a "do not resuscitate" order because he had never wanted to be on life support. I called Jace down from upstairs and asked if he remembered how we'd said that Poppy would be his angel on earth or in heaven. I said that he was in heaven now.

Jace's response was unbelievably calm and serene. "So Poppy is an angel now," he said. "So if I have a problem, Poppy can help me." He took the phone from Jewel's hand and said, "You won't need this. You can talk to everybody in heaven."

Eventually Jace broke down, but I think it was because everyone around him was breaking down. Overall, he handled the loss of his beloved father amazingly well. On the other hand, I was in shock for the following two or three months. It had been less than a week since I'd found out we were at the end. It didn't seem like it could be real.

The authorization for the treatment at Duke came two days later, on May 26th. Of course, there's no way to know if that treatment would have helped, but the timing was bitterly ironic.

***

Jewel's funeral was held on Friday, May 29th, 2020. It's hard for me to remember much from that day or the days before and after it. I was numb with shock. Somehow I got up and dressed myself and Jace that morning, but I don't know if I had even eaten in the five days since he had passed.

At that point, the entire state was locked down because of COVID-19. We weren't allowed to have more than 50 people at the funeral, and we couldn't do a service at our church. However, we found ourselves in good hands with the people at Heartswell Funeral Home in Hattiesburg, where the service was held. They did an immaculate job creating a video presentation with photos from our life. Although everything surrounding Jewel's funeral is a blur to me, I'll never forget the degree of support and care they showed us.

Honor guards performed at the service, and our neighbor prepared food. The attendees included our immediate family, one of our neighbors, and the preacher from our church in Charlotte. Many members of the South Carolina police department showed up. Some were allowed to come inside the chapel, and the ones who weren't sat in their cars and watched the service on their phones. The boys and I wore Jewel's favorite color, blue, and the boys wore silly socks, because it was our tradition to wear them on Christmas. These small things made one of the hardest moments of our lives slightly more bearable.

SHATTERED NOT BROKEN

On the way from the funeral home to the cemetery where Jewel and I have a joint mausoleum, there was a huge police processional. In addition to the police from South Carolina, there were 75 police cars from North Carolina. It was a modified COVID-era version of the sendoff that Jewel was due—scaled back, but still grand nonetheless. Before I could get back to the house, people were calling and texting about what a nice ceremony it was and how elegant everything was.

En route from the funeral home to the cemetery, we had to pass the cancer center where Jewel had his treatments. During the course of all of our trips there, he and I had found a shortcut, going a back way into the parking garage. When we passed it, I was filled with an overwhelming feeling of defeat. I remembered the beginning of the journey, when the doctor had told us that Jewel had the most curable kind of cancer, and yet, somehow, we had ended up here.

When we reached the cemetery, my parents had to come get me out of my car. I remember feeling that getting out of that car and partaking in the ceremony was the grand finale. After this, there would be no more.

The officers honored Jewel with a 21-gun salute. I thanked them when they presented me with the shell casings, but afterward, I told the preacher that I felt like each of those shells had gone into my body. Although I've never been shot, I could only imagine that the sensation would be like what I was experiencing. Everything had happened so fast. I had been working from home during lockdown, so

I'd been with him every day. How could I not have known? I felt as if both he and I had been betrayed by the doctors, given false expectations and false hopes.

I also wrestled with my faith. I said to God, "Really? What did we do?" I couldn't understand it. When Jewel had initially been diagnosed, he had cried because he didn't want Jace to experience what he had experienced with the loss of his father at such a young age. He desperately wanted to see his youngest son graduate from high school. Jewel lost his dad when he was 11, and he ended up dying when Jace was only eight.

Later, when I finally requested his medical records, I learned that the doctor had told him he'd reached the end of the road at the appointment on March 4th. I was upset that Jewel had withheld that from me, but I also came to understand it. My husband took pride in taking care of everything. He would pump gas, wash the car, make dinner, and fix everything in the house. That was the essence of who he was. For him, living in a state in which he could not do those things would not truly be living.

Although I am still working toward finding peace with what happened, time and grief counseling have allowed me to finally stop blaming myself and attain some level of clarity and understanding.

10

RISING FROM THE ASHES (2020–PRESENT)

After Jewel passed, Jace and I started spending a lot of time at the homestead. Being there in nature, seeing the goats, chickens, ducks, and geese, helped him as we grieved our loss. He started horseback riding the month after Jewel's death, and now he has three horses that he rides consistently. He also loves fishing with my dad. Jace has always had a strong bond with his grandfather, and it has grown stronger since Jewel's passing. My husband was the constant male presence in Jace's life, and now that he's gone, my dad helps to fill that void.

Our home in Charlotte was two hours away from the homestead, so whenever we went there, we'd have to leave early to allow time for the drive back. That was hard on Jace, especially when the family was all together and we would have to leave early. Eventually, he asked me if we could move closer to them. After some prayer and meditation, I agreed, and in August, we moved to Lexington, South Carolina.

In the wake of the move, I braced myself for a traumatic year. Jace was only 18 months old when we moved to Charlotte, so it was the only home he'd known. But as it turned out, there was no need to worry. He has thrived in every way. He's doing better than ever in math, learning Mandarin, and making new friends. He's gone from making As and Bs in school to bringing home report cards with straight As. (It probably helps that my parents reward him with five dollars for every A and three dollars for every B.) He does Taekwondo, which he's been doing since he was three, and last fall he joined the drumline at his school. I was particularly happy about that, because he's usually shy and reserved about any kind of performance.

The move was also good for me. Until we left Charlotte, I didn't realize that I needed a change, too. I had found myself avoiding the room in our house where Jewel had taken his last breaths, and it wasn't healthy for me. Moving to a new home in a new location allowed me to move forward with my own mental and emotional healing.

***

Since Jewel's death, Jace and I have received support from several different groups of people. Jewel's colleagues from his career in law enforcement have been extremely attentive. The ceremony in New York was a wonderful display of their care and respect for him. The day after we returned home, Fedex delivered two dozen roses and a dozen chocolate-covered strawberries from the NYPD detectives' union for Mother's Day.

Our church in Charlotte has been amazing, too. That church made Charlotte feel like home when Jewel and Jace and I moved there in 2013, and since Jewel's death, they have reached out often, sending cards and food and calling and texting to check in on me. We still drive up for services on Sundays or attend online.

My cousins have been a crucial support system. Even though none of us lives on the homestead anymore, our network is as strong as ever. We have a cousin text thread with everyone on it, and we chat on it every morning, joking around and lifting each other up. If anything happens to someone in our family, it's almost like a competition to see who can get to the homestead to help first. Right now, one of our uncles has lung cancer, so we take turns making meals for him and my aunt so he can focus on getting better. My older cousins Loretta and Linda, both of whom are cancer survivors, were a huge help to me during Jewel's cancer battle, because they understood it from his perspective.

Most of my cousins joined the military after high school, and they were all deployed to different parts of the world. Although they have all seen action, thankfully, no one was killed or injured or has suffered from lasting effects. There have been mental challenges, but we Hamptons are strong; with each other's support, we can handle those.

None of my father's siblings who lived on the homestead when I was a kid have moved away. Three have passed on, but their spouses are still there. Even though no one in my generation lives there as adults, we all treasure it. We love taking our kids there to recapture the feeling of our childhood. When we're there, we feel like our children can be free.

***

In late 2020, I made the decision to retire. When Jewel died, my supervisor had told me to take two paid months off, and during that time, I realized that, although I loved my work, it no longer made financial sense for me to stay. More importantly, I knew that I needed to stop working so I could be entirely present for Jace.

It wasn't an easy decision. I felt like I could sense other people watching me to see how I would handle my new reality. Until he became sick, Jewel was Jace's primary caregiver, and even while he was battling cancer, we parented together. When he died, I was suddenly a single parent. What we once did as a team, I would now have to do on my own. That was daunting, and I doubted myself for a while. Would I be able to care for Jace as well as Jewel did? Could I make a grilled cheese sandwich as well as he could? Could I consistently be at Jace's school to pick him up at the right time so he wouldn't have to wait? Would Jace's teachers and the school faculty get to know me the way they had always known Jewel?

The adjustment hasn't been easy. There have been moments when I have wanted to give up. But God has shown me that He wouldn't have given me this child if He didn't know I could take care of him. When I questioned whether retiring was the right thing to do, support poured in and reassured me that it was.

Over the past two years, I have often thought about my grandmother. No one would deny that my granddaddy was the backbone of their household when he was alive: Grandmother took care of the children, which was no small feat with a household of that size, but she never worked outside of their home. When he passed, I think some people expected her to crumple, but she persevered and grew stronger. I have looked to the way she responded to Granddaddy's death as inspiration, because I feel like some people expected me to crumple, too. Instead, I, too, have persevered and grown stronger.

***

Even though Jewel is gone, he is still very present in my life. Jace and I talk about Poppy every day, so that keeps his memory alive in our home, but Jewel also has a way of letting me know he's proud of me as I navigate life without him.

A few months ago, when Jace and I were in New York for the memorial service, I had a vivid dream about him on the morning of his birthday. In the dream, he tapped me and said I was on his side of the bed. Even though it was a dream, his embrace and his presence felt so real. I believe that he knew my heart was heavy, and he knew it would help me to be with him, if only for a moment in my dreams.

I often feel a sense of approval from him when I take on hard tasks. The other day, there was some caulk coming out of our sink. I asked myself, "What would Jewel Jenkins do?", and in a moment, I had the answer. I went to Home Depot, got what I needed, and fixed that caulk myself. I was proud of myself, and I could sense him looking down at me, saying, "My girl's got it."

Gradually, that has helped me gain confidence. The purchase of our house in South Carolina was a huge step forward for me. Doing that on my own helped assure me that I could move forward with things I have wanted to do in order to continue Jewel's legacy. One of those things is the scholarship I've started.

Back when Jace was born, Jewel and I started talking about creating a scholarship as a family. It would be awarded to a high school senior who was going to pursue a college degree in criminal justice or some kind of legal studies. This year, I have finally made that dream a reality—2022 was the first year the Jewels of Life scholarship was issued.

We award $500 to one student in North Carolina and one student in South Carolina. It's limited to the areas where Jewel and I have lived or that have been important in our lives: Columbia and Sumter in South Carolina and Charlotte and Harrisburg in North Carolina. It's open to individuals in those cities with a GPA of at least 3.0 who are going into those areas of study.

My hope is that the scholarship will honor Jewel's 30-year career in law enforcement and forever keep his name in people's minds and thoughts.

***

Over the course of Jewel's illness, my faith was tested to its limits. Many times, I questioned God. When Jewel passed, I truly could not understand why He would take an eight-year-old's father. And yet, it's Jace who God tends to speak through when I feel like I can't find those answers. I try not to let Jace see when I'm feeling particularly sad or really missing Jewel, but in those moments, he has a way of showing me that Jewel is still near.

One day he said to me, "Mommy, God makes no mistakes. Do you realize the number of trips we've been on since Poppy passed? When he was sick, we couldn't travel because he couldn't be around people. Now we can travel and go and do normal things."

When I heard that, I looked up at the heavens and thanked God for giving me the answer. I thought, "I get it, God. This is your way of letting him be a regular child."

That was a turning point for me. It helped me understand how important it is that Jace can now have a normal life and travel and go to birthday parties. It's the kind of life he deserves. Even though he only has one parent now, his memory of his father is strong and beautiful.

Jewel Bobby, Kristopfer, and Jace are all part of Jewel's legacy. In some ways, Jace is so much like his father. His mannerisms are so much like Jewel's that sometimes it's uncanny. And the boys carry on parts of their father as well. Because of Jewel, I am indelibly connected to my bonus sons. They look to me for guidance, and I honor that and hold it as a place to hold sacred and true.

I still miss Jewel desperately. But when I look into the eyes of Jace and the older boys, I know everything is going to be OK. When Jewel died, I was broken into a million pieces, but those pieces are being glued together again. In spite of the heartbreak, my life goes on. Like the phoenix, I am rising from the ashes.

Superman, heroic, is my Dad. This logo represents everything of my Dad's life and strength. - Jewel Bobby

SHATTERED NOT BROKEN

I chose this logo because I felt that it represents Dad's simplistic, cool, and collected nature. - Kristofer Matthew

The diamond is Daddy. Daddy was always on a pedestal. - Jace Xavier

StoryTerrace

www.ingramcontent.com/pod-product-compliance
Lightning Source LLC
LaVergne TN
LVHW061625070526
838199LV00070B/6580